FAMOUS PEOPLE
FAMOUS LIVES

Biographies of famous people to
support the curriculum.

Hans Christian Andersen

by Emma Fischel
Illustrations by Nick Ward

W
FRANKLIN WATTS
NEW YORK • LONDON • SYDNEY

First published in 1999 by
Franklin Watts
96 Leonard Street
London
EC2A 4XD

Franklin Watts Australia
14 Mars Road
Lane Cove
NSW 2066

ISBN: 0 7496 3535 5

A CIP catalogue record for this book is
available from the British Library.

Dewey Decimal Classification Number: 823

10 9 8 7 6 5 4 3 2 1

Series editor: Sarah Ridley

Printed in Great Britain

Hans Christian Andersen

"What will our little Hans do in life?" wondered his father.

"He will make shoes, or chairs or other useful things," his mother said. "That's what poor boys do!"

Hans Christian Andersen born 2 April 1805 Odense Denmark.

Hans was born into a very poor family. He grew up in a tiny house – all the family lived, ate and slept in just one room.

His father made shoes – though not very well. His mother could hardly read and write.

Ouch!

But Hans would grow up to write some of the most famous fairy tales ever known.

Life was very different 200 years ago. There were no cars, no televisions – and not many toys for a poor boy.

In the summer, Hans and his father went for long walks in the countryside.

In the long snowy winters, Hans would lie in bed and make up stories about things in the room.

Hans loved visiting his
grandmother in the
hospital where she worked.

She, and some of the other old
women there, would tell him
exciting stories hour after hour.

His father read to Hans too,
whenever he could.

"Get educated," he said to
Hans. "I never did, but
you should."

But Hans didn't do very well
at school.

9

Other children thought Hans
was strange and they often
teased him.

So Hans spent a lot of time
playing on his own.

"Hans is not an ordinary boy," said his mother.

"He is clever," said his father. "He can do anything!"

Sadly, when Hans was eleven his father died.

Hans loved singing and by the time he was thirteen he often sang for rich people in Odense.

They gave Hans money and sweets but he asked them to lend him books too.

Hans loved acting as well. He spent a lot of time helping out at the theatre in Odense. In the end, they gave him a tiny part in a play.

Scarlet tights! Now I'm a real actor!

And that gave Hans an idea.

"Now I'm fourteen I shall go to Copenhagen and become a famous actor!" Hans said.

Plenty of people told Hans what they thought of his idea.

"You have no job to go to, no friends there, and no money," said his mother. "Don't go!"

But Hans didn't listen to anyone.

Hans had never been anywhere
as big as Copenhagen before.

"So many people!" he said.
"And soon they will all know
my name!"

Straight away, Hans went to see the most famous dancer in all of Denmark, Madame Schall.

"I'd like a job, please," he said to her. "I can do lots of clever things. Watch!"

Madame Schall just told him to go away.

For three years Hans struggled to make a living in Copenhagen as a singer, dancer and actor.

He had little bits of work – and lots of disappointments.

Some of the other actors were unkind to him as well.

PROGRAMME
TROLL- Hans Andersen
HERO:
THR:

19

"I won't give up!" said Hans. And he did manage to find people to help him.

By now he had started to write poems and plays. He read them to anyone who would listen.

"Marvellous," people said. But then they laughed at him behind his back.

This poem is very good indeed!

More nonsense! How strange he is!

Hans was very poor and almost always hungry.

The third winter was the coldest and loneliest of all. He nearly starved to death.

Just look at him — so big and peculiar.

Still he struggled on and wrote
another play.

"About your play…" said Jonas Collin, the Director of the Royal Theatre.

"Is it good?" asked Hans.

"No!" said Jonas. "It's rubbish But I think you'll write something good one day!"

"So what should I do now?" asked Hans.

"Go back to school and continue to learn," said Jonas. "It's never too late!"

At the age of seventeen
Hans went back to school.

He was miserable there a lot of
the time, and the head teacher
bullied him horribly.

Stop snivelling,
beanpole!

Hans wrote a lot to his new friend and his new friend wrote back.

And after six years Hans passed all his exams.

Hans was twenty-two, and he felt confident when he went back to Copenhagen.

But nothing went smoothly. Again and again, Hans had success...

...and then failure.

Still Hans wrote and wrote —
and read aloud. Even his friends
got fed up in the end.

"You're making a fool of
yourself. You're writing too
much, too fast," they said.
"Go away. See new places!"

The King of Denmark gave
Hans some money and Hans
went travelling for almost
two years.

While Hans was away his mother died. Then there was yet more bad news about his writing.

"He will give up!" said some, but he didn't. Instead, he wrote another book when he came home. And that was when things started to change.

PUBLISHERS

The IMPROVISATORE by Hans Andersen.

The publishers like this one!

Hans had another idea too – a story for children to read. It was called *The Tinderbox* and was all about a witch, a soldier and three fierce dogs.

He wrote three more soon after, and then still more.

"They are perfect," said a friend. "They are your best writing ever."

But Hans wasn't so sure.

"What are these tales?" said the critics. "He has written them as if he were speaking them to a child! That's no way to do it!"

"I knew it," said Hans. "I'm no good at children's stories, either."

But there were some people who thought he was very good indeed.

No boring bits to do us good!

No long words!

No teaching!

We love them!

It's as if you are there telling them to us!

Dear Mr Hans Andersen a little girl likes your fairytales very much Ethel Weguelin - London

Hans was a success at last! He wrote 156 fairy tales in all.

"I never dreamed it would be these tales for children that made me famous!" he said.

THE Emperor's New Clothes

Now Hans was forty and all his books were doing well.

From now on he spent his time
writing and travelling.
Everywhere he went in Europe
he met famous writers and artists.

"Visit me!" said kings and queens all over Europe.

"And me," said dukes and duchesses.

Hans loved his lifestyle but he never forgot what it was like to be poor and hungry, or laughed at and teased.

'Look how ugly he is!'

'Her little hands were numb with cold.'

Hans was sixty-two now.

"You are the best-loved writer in all Denmark," said the people of Odense. "Let us honour you."

"The son of a shoemaker has become famous throughout the world. This then is a real fairy tale come true!" the people said.

And when Hans died at the age of seventy, all the bells of Copenhagen rang out for him.

Further facts

Hans as a child

There was so little space in the house Hans grew up in that he was put to sleep in his parents' big bed. When they wanted to go to bed they let down a wooden bench that was hinged up against the wall, made up a bed and moved him, sleeping, onto it.

Paper cuts

Hans was amazingly good at cutting little figures out of paper. He created a student character in his story *Little Ida's Flowers*, who enchants a girl, Ida, with his pictures cut out of paper and his wonderful story of her flowers.

Hans's garden

Hans had a little garden – in the gutter between the roof of his house and the next! His mother grew herbs and vegetables in pots there. Hans writes about it in *The Snow Queen* where Key and Gerda sit on little stools in the gutter between their houses.

Odense prison

Once Hans went with his parents to dinner with the jailer at Odense prison. There was more delicious food there than he would ever have at home – but Hans couldn't eat a thing. He had scared himself too much pretending he was in a robber's castle!

Important dates in Hans Christian Andersen's lifetime

1802   Hans is born in Odense, Denmark.

1816   Hans's father dies.

1819   Hans goes to Copenhagen to become an actor.

1822   Hans meets Jonas Collin and goes to Slagelse grammar school.

1829   Hans's first successful travel book is published. His first play is put on.

1831   Hans spends two years travelling, mostly in Germany, France and Italy.

1835   *The Improvisatore* is published, followed by two more novels.

1835   Hans writes his first fairy tale, *The Tinderbox*.

1837   Hans writes *The Little Mermaid* and *The Emperor's New Clothes*.

1843   Hans writes *The Ugly Duckling*.

1845   Hans writes *The Snow Queen*.

1847   Hans visits England and Scotland. He meets Charles Dickens.

1855   Hans writes a book about his life.

1857   Hans visits London and stays with Dickens. He travels a lot from now on.

1862   Hans's *Fairy Tales and Stories* are published in one big book for the first time.

1872   Hans's last fairy tales are published.

1875   Hans dies while staying at a friend's house.